THE GREAT HUNGER

THE GALLANT JOHN-JOE

The Great Hunger

The Gallant John-Joe

TOM MAC INTYRE

THE LILLIPUT PRESS
DUBLIN

This edition first published 2002 by
THE LILLIPUT PRESS LTD
62–63 Sitric Road, Arbour Hill,
Dublin 7, Ireland
www.lilliputpress.ie

The Great Hunger: Poem into Play, comprising Patrick Kavanagh's
poem 'The Great Hunger' and Tom Mac Intyre's play of the same
name, with commentary by Antoinette Quinn, Patrick Mason and
Vincent Hurley, was published by Lilliput in 1988.

A CIP record for this title is available from
The British Library.

1 3 5 7 9 10 8 6 4 2

ISBN 1 901866 83 1

*The Lilliput Press receives financial assistance from
An Chombairle Ealaíon / The Arts Council of Ireland.*

Set by Marsha Swan in Hoefler Text
Printed by Betaprint, Clonshaugh, Dublin, Ireland

CONTENTS

The Great Hunger

for Tom Hickey

Setting

Loosely defined, fluid as possible. Three main areas. Outdoors is placed centrally – it is marked only by a wooden gate, far upstage. The kitchen and chapel areas: place downstage left and right, respectively. THE MOTHER will usually be found in the kitchen area; place there, also, a large black kettle and a bucket. The chapel is distinguished by a tabernacle resting on its pedestal.

Duration

A little over one hundred minutes; the piece is played, ideally, without an interval.

Participants

MAGUIRE
THE MOTHER (a wooden effigy)
THE SISTER, MARY ANNE
THE PRIEST
AGNES
THE SCHOOL-GIRL
TOM MALONE
PACKY
JOE
EXTRA MALE
YOUNG WOMEN

The piece may be played by six players, three female and three male.

Scene One

Wind sounds, harsh. Fading as MAGUIRE *appears.* MAGUIRE *wandering the space ...*

MAGUIRE: The bridge is too narrow ... The bridge is too narrow and the hay has wings.

PACKY (*off*): Maguire ... Maguire ...

MAGUIRE: And thirty-five could take the sparrow's bow ...

PACKY: Maguire ... Maguire ...

MAGUIRE: You're wrong ... You're wrong about that thing I was tellin' you, you're wrong, you're wrong ...

PACKY: Maguire ... Maguire ...

MAGUIRE: The tubs is white ... The tubs is white ... The tubs is white ...

PACKY *enters upstage right with lantern, lit. Crosses upstage of the gate to exit upstage left.*

PACKY: Maguire, you're wrong about that thing I was tellin' you, Maguire, you're wrong, you're wrong ...

MAGUIRE: We ought to be finished by the morrow ...

MAGUIRE *looks about him as if coming out of sleep, removes glasses, wipes eyes with closed fists, enters the daylight world.*

Scene Two

Two of MAGUIRE's *men,* MALONE *and* JOE, *enter upstage left. They carry spades, and, between them, a metal bath. It contains three metal buckets and a bag-apron. The bath is set downstage left, as is the bag-apron.* MALONE *and* JOE *go to the head of the potato drills where* MAGUIRE *joins them. The buckets have been distributed. The potato-picking commences.*

PACKY *has also entered upstage left, and settled on the gate. From there he watches the action.*

Girlish laughter off. The men give no heed.

MAGUIRE *erupts. Something spotted in the next field. He whistles for the dog. No dog to be had.*

MAGUIRE: Curse o' God, where's that dog? Never where he's wanted.

A burst of shouting from MAGUIRE, *and wild mime of pegging stones. As they work, the three converse.*

MAGUIRE: Move forward the basket—
JOE: The wind's over Brannigan's—
MAGUIRE: Balance it steady—
JOE: That means rain—
MALONE: Down the ruckety pass—
MAGUIRE: The wind's over Brannigan's—
JOE: That means rain—
MALONE: Down the ruckety pass—
MAGUIRE: Pull down the shafts of that cart, Joe—

JOE: And straddle the horse—

MAGUIRE: And straddle the horse—

MALONE: Down the ruckety pass—

MAGUIRE: Graip up some withered stalks, graip up some withered stalks and see that no potato fails—

JOE: Over the tailboard—

MAGUIRE: Over the tailboard—

MALONE: Down the ruckety pass—

MAGUIRE: Going down the ruckety pass. And that's a job, that's a job we'll have to do in December—

JOE: Gravel it—

MAGUIRE: Gravel it and build a kerb—

MALONE: Down the ruckety pass—

JOE: And build a kerb—

MAGUIRE: Gravel it and build a kerb on the bog side—

MALONE: On the bog side—

Burst of girlish laughter off, and one runs on, downstage right, 'Will-I-won't-I' demeanour. Runs downstage of the men to leapfrog over JOE, *and – full tilt – exit upstage left.*

The heads of the men dive – three heads hanging between wide-apart legs – to see. Too late. Slowly they rise from that position and become scarecrows stirring lightly in the wind, scarecrows that swivel and stare vacantly into the audience.

PACKY, *watcher on the gate, chants.*

PACKY: Ploughs and sows ... Eats fresh food ... Loves fresh women ... His own master – can talk to God.

The men at work again, bringing the full buckets to empty the potatoes into the bath.

MAGUIRE: Never where he's wanted—

MALONE *and* JOE *exit upstage right with bath, buckets, spades.* PACKY *is exiting upstage left as* MAGUIRE *playfully skelps a couple of potatoes off the back wall.* MAGUIRE *dons his bag-apron and moves downstage right as* MARY ANNE *enters stage right.*

Scene Three

MAGUIRE: Patrick Maguire went home and made cocoa ... The sister, the sister – hens and calves, calves and hens ...

MARY ANNE *arrives downstage left carrying a large black kettle and an enamel bucket containing water. She leaves down kettle and bucket and moves to a position upstage and stage right of* THE MOTHER. *She stares* MAGUIRE *who's still downstage right.* MAGUIRE *responds by crossing to* THE MOTHER *and making an irritated attempt to loosen the cord which binds the cover about her.* MARY ANNE *turns her back on him, faces upstage.* MAGUIRE *moves downstage to occupy himself pouring water from bucket to kettle. The two share another look.* MAGUIRE *approaches* THE MOTHER. *A second time, claws at the cord. Fails to loosen it.* MARY ANNE *intervenes, sweeps towards him with scissors aloft, snips. Returns to her position, again gives her back to the proceedings.*

The cord is now in MAGUIRE's *control. He loosens it all the way by running circles about* THE MOTHER. *Cord free, and dumped on the ground.*

MAGUIRE *gives his attention to the cover, frees it – but not without making work for himself. Flings sheet on the ground in turn.*

MARY ANNE *spins to face him. Goes forward to gather cord and cover – briskly, neatly – and places both downstage in line with bucket and kettle. That done, she returns to her position upstage of* THE MOTHER. *She again faces upstage but her stance is mitigated. A hint of the diagonal gives her a sightline to the downstage left area.*

The MOTHER-*effigy contains a drawer.* MAGUIRE *opens it, takes out a wire brush and a duster. He throws the brush to* MARY ANNE. *She catches it, moves downstage left and starts cleaning the kettle, first removing the lid.*

MAGUIRE *busies himself cleaning* THE MOTHER's *face, talking to her at the start, shouting before long.*

MAGUIRE: No, no, the pig-gelder Nallon—
MARY ANNE: What's keeping you? Did you let the hens out you?
MAGUIRE: No—
MARY ANNE: Did you open the barn door? Let the young calves in?
MAGUIRE: The pig-gelder, the pig-gelder—
MARY ANNE: What's *he* looking for there?
MAGUIRE: *Nallon*—
MARY ANNE: Brazil and the Amazon—
MAGUIRE: The pig-gelder Nallon—
MARY ANNE: Brazil and the Amazon—
MAGUIRE: The pig-gelder Nallon—
MARY ANNE: Poor Paddy Maguire—
MAGUIRE: *Nallon*—

MARY ANNE: The great cattle-dealer hobo—
MAGUIRE: Nallon, *Nallon, Nallon*—

MAGUIRE *pitches the duster into the drawer, kicks the drawer shut.*
MARY ANNE *slams the lid on the kettle and throws the wire brush to*
MAGUIRE. *He catches it. Extended pause as they stare each other.*
MAGUIRE *then to the drawer. Opens it, tosses the wire brush into it, closes*
the drawer. Looks again at MARY ANNE.

MARY ANNE *will not be rushed. She stoops, rests her hands on the kettle,*
releases a sigh.

MAGUIRE, *downstage right of* THE MOTHER, *flops to the floor, sits with*
his back to THE MOTHER, *legs extended, repetitively banging his feet*
together. He converses with MARY ANNE *by that mode.*

She converses with him by her mode of pouring water very slowly from
bucket to kettle. Squeaks from the bucket handle are an aid to articula-
tion. She takes forever at pouring the water.

Bucket empty, MARY ANNE *replaces lid on kettle, settles kettle and bucket*
and cord and cover, moves upstage to THE MOTHER, *checks* THE
MOTHER'*s face, and exits downstage left. During that series of move-*
ments, she communes with herself.

MARY ANNE: Pigs and cows, Punch and Judy ... Punch and Judy,
pigs and cows ... Nallon ... The pig-gelder Nallon...

MAGUIRE *senses her exit, stops his feet-banging. Listens. Rises and goes to*
the drawer. Opens it. Interrupts himself to remove the bag-apron and place
it downstage, a prayer-mat of sorts. Returns to the drawer, takes from it a

bellows. With the bellows, goes to the bag-apron. Kneels. Tentatively works the bellows, then works it to climax in an image of masturbation.

He returns the bellows to the drawer, shuts the drawer. Goes to the kettle and pours from the kettle back into the bucket, pouring that releases The Isle of Capri *on the sound track. Quality of the recording to suggest the uncertain radio in the farmhouse back of the hills.*

Scene Four

Enter MALONE *upstage right, waltzing to the music. He settles upstage of the gate, leaning across it.* MAGUIRE *joins him there.* MAGUIRE *playfully belts* MALONE *with his cap, and there's a dance between them which develops that greeting. Finally, the two yield to the enjoyment of staring into emptiness.*

Three YOUNG WOMEN *enter, variously, settle downstage right. Vivaciously, they daub their mouths with lipstick, perfume themselves. The three play with these phrases:* If he opens his eyes ... if he opens, opens, opens ... sight is sin ... if he opens legs ... a face in the crust ... legs, legs, legs ...

MAGUIRE *and* MALONE, *swiping at midges, have turned their backs to the action. As the* YOUNG WOMEN *get into their stride,* AGNES *declaims—*

AGNES: Sittin' on a wooden gate, sittin' on a wooden gate, sittin' on a wooden gate, he didn't give a damn ... Said whatever came into his head, said whatever came into his head, said whatever came into his head, he didn't give a damn.

THE PRIEST *enters upstage right, a fraction after the* YOUNG WOMEN, *and makes for the downstage left area. First he goes to the kettle, taps it several times with polished toe. Next the bucket. He stoops, taken by his reflection in the water, adjusts his collar.*

Now he approaches THE MOTHER. *He studies her. Takes out a small mirror and holds it to her mouth. The breath-stain is faint, it seems ... He moves his index finger across her line of vision. Yes, she's alive. He takes off his hat and rests it on her lap. He goes to her right ear and bawls into it. We hear nothing. Repeat. This time we hear.*

THE PRIEST: Your children will miss you when you're gone.

At intervals, MAGUIRE *and* MALONE *flail at the midges, fall into their torpor again.*

THE PRIEST *now turns entertainer, does a card-trick for* THE MOTHER. *He offers a running commentary of sounds rather than words. Card-trick over,* THE PRIEST *gives himself to listening, head bowed, to* THE MOTHER. *A confession moment, could be. Thus positioned,* THE PRIEST *falls asleep.*

The moment of THE PRIEST's *dropping off brings* PACKY *racing on, blades of grass held to his lips to form a makeshift whistle – which he works to resonant effect. He delivers a blast to the tabernacle, a blast to* THE MOTHER, *then races off.*

The YOUNG WOMEN *respond to his incursion by placing their palms, crossed, in front of their faces. His exit releases them. They jump to their feet and flash lights over the audience from hand-mirrors they manoeuvre. Next they flash the mirrors at* MAGUIRE *and* MALONE *upstage of the gate. And they shout at the men.*

YOUNG WOMEN: What's keeping you? And the cows to be milked and all the other work there's to do. We'll not stay here all night.

They exit, variously. One of them, noticing THE PRIEST'S *hat on the lap of* THE MOTHER, *grabs it and slaps it on* THE MOTHER'S *head.*

The teasing of the YOUNG WOMEN *stirs* MAGUIRE *and* MALONE *to further flailing at the midges, no more than that.*

THE PRIEST *rouses from his sleep. Looks about him. Spots his hat on the head of* THE MOTHER. *Smiles for her. Takes his hat and dons it. Speaks to* THE MOTHER.

THE PRIEST: The likes of you this parish never knew.

He exits upstage right.

MAGUIRE *and* MALONE *stir themselves.* MAGUIRE *takes out a cigarette and lights up.* MALONE – *gasping for a drag* – *cadges a cigarette. The pair puff contentedly.*

The summer evening light yields to night. Glow of the cigarettes by the gate, glow of one cigarette answering the other, that conversation.

The two make for home.

MAGUIRE: Is that a ghost or a tree?
MALONE: Down the ruckety pass—

MAGUIRE: Duffy's place is very convenient.
MALONE: A wonderful night we had.

MAGUIRE *and* MALONE *exit downstage right.*

Scene Five

A spring moment of release. Brilliant lighting, triumphant music – but finding its way, prelude as yet. MALONE *enters downstage right,* PACKY *upstage left. They each carry piles of green-leaved branches which they dump centre-stage. And off.*

Now all the players – bar THE PRIEST *– enter and take possession of the branches. The green branch is magic. For each an individual way of dealing with it.* MAGUIRE *is ecstatic,* MARY ANNE *severe.* THE SCHOOL-GIRL *is rapt, squeezing the leaves, raising her hand to drink the odours;* AGNES *lies down and, laughing, strokes the branches against thighs, breasts, face;* MALONE *is tearing off leaves, pocketing them happily;* PACKY *finds gestures at once grotesque and fragile to convey his delight.*

A tremendous stir and the music rising in intensity. MAGUIRE, MARY ANNE, *and* MALONE *fuss about* THE MOTHER. *A branch for her also. The cover – as rug – about her shoulders. Procession imminent. The music peaks, and they process about the space.* THE SCHOOL-GIRL *dips her branch in the bucket, blesses each player in turn, blesses the audience.*

THE SCHOOL-GIRL: Holy Spirit is the rising sap ... Holy Spirit is the rising sap ...

The space is drumming exuberance.

THE PRIEST *enters downstage right. Everything stops.* THE PRIEST *removes the cover from the tabernacle. The players discard the branches and assemble (*THE MOTHER *is brought along) in the 'chapel' area, kneeling positions.*

PACKY, *as altar-boy, is downstage right, close to* THE PRIEST. AGNES *is in the 'front row', flirtatious in her concentration on* THE PRIEST. *Next comes* MARY ANNE *and* THE MOTHER. *Thereafter,* THE SCHOOL-GIRL, MALONE, *and, downstage left,* MAGUIRE.

To start, there's an orchestrated din of coughing which turns to a chorale of farmyard noises, animal and fowl. This rises wildly so that THE PRIEST *is forced to exercise control. A signal to* PACKY, *and* PACKY *jingles a minatory bell. The din subsides.*

Prayers: from the dialogue snippets below, surreal antiphonal exchanges are developed between THE PRIEST *and the congregation, and between members of the congregation.*

Remember Eileen Farrelly? I was thinking a man might do a
   damn sight worse.

She ought to give a crop if any land gives.

Wonder should I cross-plough that turnip ground?

Is that Cassidy's ass out in my clover?

The wind's over Brannigan's, that means rain.

Did you part with your filly, Jack?

Kate, throw another sod on that fire.

Get out, you little tramps.

Easy there, Fanny, easy pet.

Back in, back in, and you'll have all the luck.

Curse o' God, where's that dog?

Drive slower with the foal mare, Joe.

My turnips are destroyed with the blackguardly crows.

Hop back there, Polly, hoy back, woa, wae *[used as reiterated 'Amen'].*

A precise signal from THE PRIEST *concludes prayers. He allows a silence to shape. Searches in the folds of his vestments for the tabernacle key. Roots in his pockets. Key not to be found – until an embarrassed* PACKY *produces it from his pocket.* THE PRIEST *(with a look of chastisement for* PACKY*) takes the key, kisses it. Addresses himself to the tabernacle door. Insertion of the key in the lock. Turning of the key. Opening of the door. Curtains of red silk visible. Delicately,* THE PRIEST *parts these. He takes out a small dingy chalice, tarnished, but it contains the mystery. He extends it to the congregation. Worshipful, they yield.*

Break, on the tinkle of a bell from PACKY.

A nod from THE PRIEST *sends* MAGUIRE *into action with the long-handled collection-box. Each contribution is individualized.* AGNES *releases her coins like delectable confections for the priest.* MARY ANNE *defines constriction: tight-lipped. A single coin.* THE SCHOOL-GIRL *becomes a Jack-in-the-Box to* MAGUIRE's *conducting.* MALONE *contents himself with simply rattling the box.*

Collection completed, MAGUIRE, *passing the bucket, dreamily spills all the coins into the water – as if the most natural thing in the world.*

All stare. MAGUIRE *comes to, stands there.* THE PRIEST *starts laughing – exoneration (maybe). Laughing spreads, threatens to become tumult.* THE PRIEST *cools it with a look.*

PACKY *rings the bell and the mass is over. The congregation scatter.* THE MOTHER *is taken home,* MARY ANNE, AGNES, THE SCHOOL-GIRL *and* MALONE, *the bearers.*

PACKY *hovers to assist* THE PRIEST's *disrobing.*

MAGUIRE, *rattling a coin in the collection-box, ambiguously his own man, goes up to* THE PRIEST, *gives an absent-minded genuflection, and is moving upstage left to exit when his attention is caught by* AGNES *upstage right.*

THE PRIEST *and* PACKY *are downstage right. Poised.*

AGNES *stares* MAGUIRE, *stare close to the accusatory.* MAGUIRE *is held.* AGNES *– a broad powerful gesture for* MAGUIRE's *assimilation – bangs her fist silently against the back wall. Exits upstage right.* MAGUIRE *exits upstage left.*

And THE PRIEST, PACKY *in attendance, commences disrobing. He hands* PACKY *the biretta, places the maniple on* PACKY's *left arm, robes* PACKY *in the chasuble, quizzing* PACKY *as he does.*

THE PRIEST: Who bent the coin that it stuck in the slot? The brown breeze through the thistles ... Through the thistles the brown breeze ...

THE PRIEST – *elaborately* – *removes the cincture, which he then spirals into the biretta* – PACKY *observing in fascination.*

THE PRIEST: We must not want too much to know.

On that line, THE PRIEST *pulls a card from the biretta – for* PACKY's *edification and astonishment.*

Exit PACKY *downstage right.*

THE PRIEST *faces the audience, rubs his palms, magics the card out of existence.*

Exit THE PRIEST *upstage right.*

Scene Six

THE SCHOOL-GIRL *on. She flourishes a book of raffle tickets, comes downstage shaking it like a tambourine. She writes, tears off a counter-foil, throws it to the house.*

THE SCHOOL-GIRL: For holy funds—

Now she does a figure of eight around THE MOTHER *and tabernacle, writes again, repeats the routine and the line.*

This brings MAGUIRE *on, jingling coins. She notices. She gestures – Will you buy? He will. He comes downstage to her, stands over her, as, resting on one knee, she writes, gives him the counterfoil. He takes it, and – jokey – withholds the money. He jigs about the space, teasing her and generally clowning: animal imitations, fowl imitations. Frustrated, she pitches the book of tickets at him and stalks off.*

MAGUIRE *changes tack. Shouts after her, halts her. Goes towards her and places the money on the ground and retreats – as she advances – with the book of tickets now in his possession. She collects the money. And he's off into a second round of teasing, flourishing the tickets à la* THE SCHOOL-GIRL *at the start of the scene.*

MAGUIRE'S *teasing romp takes him out of the space – but the noise of the tickets being 'rattled' suggests where he is: downstage right and off. She advances in that direction. The noise leads her on.*

She peers irritably, hesitates. And MAGUIRE *– squawking – gallops on upstage left. She screeches.* MAGUIRE *again into his fowl imitations – turkey sounds and strutting, goose-hissing and waddling, that idiom.*

THE SCHOOL-GIRL *in difficulties. She backs off, for a moment. Retaliates by taking up his idiom and challenging him with verve. So: that dance (mirror-game) with a sudden access of mutual enjoyment. The natural climax is that she leaps boldly into his embrace: her arms about his neck, her legs about his waist. The two whirl, brief release, then a jolt.*

There's a mutual realization of the sexual voltage. The pulse of this com-mands the space.

Slowly, dangerously, THE SCHOOL-GIRL *slides from* MAGUIRE'S *embrace, grabs the tickets from him and exits at speed.*

MAGUIRE *alone, adrift, recovering, not recovering.*

Scene Seven

Evening at the crossroads ... MAGUIRE *joined by* MALONE, JOE *and* PACKY. *The four commence a desultory game of pitch-and-toss – horse-play an element – which yields quickly to the following sequence: the play-ers' recollections of the Mucker Dramatic Society's last presentation, the recollections taking the shape of line-swopping with a competitive tilt.*

As the game of pitch-and-toss disintegrates, MARY ANNE *enters down-stage left and hunkers by* THE MOTHER. *She has a jar of Pond's Cold Cream. Patiently, dreamily, she rubs cream on her hands and neck.*

MAGUIRE *sets the line-swopping in motion—*

MAGUIRE: God the Father ... God the Father ... God the Father
 in a tree ...?

MALONE *takes up the challenge—*

MALONE: God is in the bits ... God is in the bits ... God is in the
 bits and pieces of ...?

PACKY *is suddenly a target. The others advance demandingly on him:*
PACKY, *gawky/girlish, is there to be teased, to be murkily desired.*

MAG/MAL/JOE: Of? Of? Of? Of?
PACKY: Of every day—

Mockingly, the three interrogators echo PACKY's *'Of every day'*. PACKY
*retaliates, hesitantly shows his paces, mimes the act of breaking bread as
he challenges them to respond.*

PACKY: In a crumb of bread? In a crumb of bread? In a crumb of
    bread?

The others turn the question back on PACKY, *surrounding him, jostling
him.*

MAG/MAL/JOE: Crumb of bread? Crumb of bread? Crumb of bread?
PACKY: The whole mystery is ...

Again the others echo his answer mockingly.

MAG/MAL/JOE: The *whole* mystery is ... The *whole* mystery is ...
    The *whole* mystery is ...

*The diversion is taking on intensity, they're all more and more caught in
the rhythms of it.* MAGUIRE *keeps it moving.*

MAGUIRE: The green leaves? The green leaves? The green leaves?

*He's waving a small branch as he puts the question, jigging about invit-
ing the others to rush him, tumble him.*

MAGUIRE: The green leaves? The green leaves?

The others rush him.

MAG/MAL/JOE: The green leaves? The green leaves? The green leaves?

They tumble MAGUIRE. *He shouts the answering line as he goes down.*

MAGUIRE: Christ will be the green leaves that will come—
OMNES: Christ will be the green leaves that will come—

That's a signal. They all know the next move. MAGUIRE *– content to wait – drifts downstage, gives himself to a gestural cameo which posits the branch in his possession as the starting-handle of a car.* MALONE *and* JOE, *meanwhile, have been active by the gate. They plank* PACKY *upstage of the gate and move to re-stage the resurrection hour.* MALONE *and* JOE, *downstage right and left of the gate, produce dawn/wind sounds by whirling lengths of wire above their heads.* PACKY *has been climbing the gate. He now stands on it as the risen Christ, arms outstretched, palms spread wide – and focusing on* MAGUIRE, *even as* MAGUIRE *is turning to meet the upstage event.* MAGUIRE, *shaken, takes off his cap. All goes eerily quiet.* MALONE *and* JOE *drop the lengths of wire.* MARY ANNE *speaks into the silence.*

MARY ANNE: Your children'll miss you when you're gone.

MAGUIRE, MALONE, *and* JOE *resume the pitch-and-toss – but the air is changed.* PACKY *remains on the gate, seated.* MARY ANNE *lids the jar of Pond's cream, rises, and – diagonal line through the heedless males – makes her slow exit upstage right.*

Frail echoes of the line-swopping dialogue accompany the resumed pitch-and-toss.

MAGUIRE: God the Father in a tree—
MALONE: God is in the bits—
JOE: In a crumb of bread—
MAGUIRE: God the Father—
MALONE: In the bits—
JOE: Crumb of bread—
MAGUIRE: God—
MALONE: Bits—
JOE: Crumb—

That final 'crumb' cues the sound of a passing train. All listen, immobilized ... The sound fades. The pitch-and-toss is beyond recovery – for now.
MAGUIRE *– in an evident fever – breaks from the group and exits downstage right. The other three hold separate positions, idly brooding:* PACKY *on the gate,* MALONE *hunkered downstage right,* JOE *standing midstage left between the gate and* THE MOTHER.

MAGUIRE'S *hysterical laughter can be heard off. He spins back on, very near the edge, and careers about the space, repeating—*

MAGUIRE: Patrick Maguire went home and made cocoa ...

His whirl now finds blurred focus. He approaches PACKY *on the gate, declaring urgently—*

MAGUIRE: Patrick Maguire went home and made cocoa and broke a chunk off the loaf of wheaten bread ...

PACKY *makes no response.* MAGUIRE *descends on* JOE—

MAGUIRE: His mother called down to him to look again and make sure the hen-house was locked ...

JOE *makes no response.* MAGUIRE *descends on* MALONE —

MAGUIRE: His sister grunted in bed, the sound of a sow taking up a new position ...

MALONE *makes no response.* MAGUIRE – *more and more into vertigo – is swept wildly about the space, gabbling fragments from the speeches he has just uttered. He halts downstage right: tongue bobbing in and out, hands fluttering in the crotch area. Takes off again, distrait—*

MAGUIRE: Patrick Maguire went home and made cocoa and broke a chunk off the loaf of wheaten bread. His mother called down to him to look again and make sure the hen-house was locked. His sister grunted in bed, the sound of a sow taking up a new position ...

He comes to rest downstage left as we hear the voices of young women, gabbling easily, passing by ...

All the males listen, cling to the fading sounds. In the silence that follows, the four stare emptily across the audience and into the beyond.

They lurch free of that fog. MALONE *tosses a coin,* JOE *shoulders him playfully to the ground,* PACKY *pushes* MAGUIRE *on to* MALONE, MAGUIRE *straddles* MALONE, *and the heifer romp is away.*

MALONE *as the heifer. Commence with a general inspection, to a cacophony of groans from the animal. The teeth are checked, the flanks, the backbone is tickled – the heifer bucks madly – and, for climax, the hindquarters are feelingly caressed.*

MAGUIRE *fetches a bucket, and –* PACKY *in charge – the heifer is given a 'drink' from the bucket. More pushing and mauling and medley of sounds.*

The mounting of the heifer. As PACKY *and the heifer perform their bucket-dance,* JOE, MAGUIRE *leading him, canters the perimeter, steadies, and – the hullabaloo reaching peak – moves in and mounts the waiting heifer. This action develops into a scrum. There's a writhing of bodies and a sudden lunge for* PACKY *– who exits at speed.*

MAGUIRE: Packy ... Packy ... Packy ...

MAGUIRE, MALONE *and* JOE *rise one by one and silently. An exhausted quiet rules.* JOE *exits.* MAGUIRE *and* MALONE *adrift in the aftermath.*

MALONE: What about home?
MAGUIRE: We're too tired to go home yet.
MALONE: Are you using your double-tree this week?
MAGUIRE: Why? D'ye want it?
MALONE (*exiting*): Why? D'ye want it? Why? D'ye want it? Why? D'ye want it?

MAGUIRE *alone in the space, downstage right. Kneading crumbs of clay. His hands fall idle. He studies his hands ... lifts them fractionally for a better view ... studies his hands ...*

Scene Eight

MAGUIRE *to the gate. He whistles for the dog. No sign of the dog.*
MAGUIRE *to the kitchen area. He stands by* THE MOTHER. *Tries to artic-*
ulate something. Gives up. Opens the drawer of the MOTHER-*effigy,*
takes out a duster, wipes THE MOTHER's *eyes and nose. Tries again to*
articulate something.

MAGUIRE: Mother ... Mother ...

He puts the duster away, and, kneeling position, slowly closes the drawer.

THE SCHOOL-GIRL *enters upstage left, picks up a branch as she arrives,*
and crosses upstage of the gate to exit downstage right. She pulls leaves off
the branch as she delivers the lines.

THE SCHOOL-GIRL: The poor peasant talking to himself in a sta-
ble door, an ignorant peasant deep in dung ... Where is his sil-
ver bowl of knowledge hung? Why should men be asked to
believe in a soul that is only the mark of a hoof in guttery
gaps? A man is what is written ... A man is what is written ...

As she exits, MAGUIRE *rouses himself. He clutches* THE MOTHER, *leans*
his head on her shoulder. With his fist he beats her breast, slowly, mechan-
ically, the fist beats on the breast of THE MOTHER.

Scene Nine

*Ploughing. Abrupt switch to an atmosphere of wild release. To com-
mence: seagulls noisily active about the upturned sod. Two of the* YOUNG
WOMEN, *plus* PACKY, *each with a white table-cloth, frenetic through the
space. And screeching. The third* YOUNG WOMAN *involved at the same
tempo – but as terrier dog, fighting with the birds, with anything that
moves, helplessly taken by the excitement.*

Enter MAGUIRE *guiding the imaginary plough,* MALONE *and* JOE *as the
horses. Movement – tempestuous – back-and-forth in the space. Intricate
gymnastics negotiating the turns at each end – swerve and sway, sock
free, sock plunged again, at intervals impeded by a rock or whatever ...*

*The wheeling birds and uncontrollable dog – and the giddy horses –
intensify a persistent sense of the operation threatening to run amok.*
MAGUIRE *has shouts for the horses—*

MAGUIRE: Hop back there, Polly, hop back, woa, wae ... Easy
there, Fanny, easy pet ...

*The scene is brief and moves rapidly towards climax – the horses out of
control, and, on the heels of that,* MAGUIRE *and the horses, tangled on the
ground, 'harness' flying in all directions.*

*The seagulls vanish, their work done. The terrier – prime miscreant – delays
to piss on the prostrate* MAGUIRE, *vanishes in turn, yelping delirium.*

The horses – becoming men – laugh as they right themselves. MAGUIRE,
getting to his feet, is not amused.

MAGUIRE: It's not a bit funny ...

MAGUIRE *kicks the gate several times—*

MAGUIRE: Not a bit funny ... Not a bit funny ...

MAGUIRE *collects the 'plough' (a length of wood suffices) and the 'harness' (ropes), and places them downstage centre, catching breath, poised for the reward/relaxation of the pub.*

Scene Ten

Three pints of Guinness are waiting on a covered tray downstage right. MALONE *lifts the tray.* JOE *triumphantly removes the cover, and casually places it on* MALONE'*s head – a quasi-helmet. Taken by the picture,* JOE *remarks to* MAGUIRE—

JOE: Rommel—

MAGUIRE *agrees: there is a likeness. The three – all in possession of their pints by now – play with the word 'Rommel', testing the curiosity – and familiarity – of it. This cadence finds peak in the three raising their pints in a toast—*

OMNES: Rommel—

The three next move about in close formation, leaning against each other, manoeuvring for positions of maximum comfort before settling into a position where they are adroitly/comfortably propping each other up.

Finding the position of maximum comfort involves a deal of grunt and groan and orchestrated sigh. Finally, contentment. They savour the pints. And they converse: insider talk, seasoned with the inconsequential. MAGUIRE *leads off—*

MAGUIRE: She ought to give a crop if any land gives.
JOE: They know their geography.
MAGUIRE: No one'd take her.
MALONE: That's flat porter.

They drink.

JOE: Me turnips—
MALONE: 'Turnips!'
JOE: Me turnips is destroyed with the blackguardly crows.
MAGUIRE: Another one.
MALONE: That's flat porter.

They jostle for more comfort, settle again.

MAGUIRE: Stand for no nonsense—
JOE: There's rogues—
MAGUIRE: Your filly, Jack—
JOE: There's rogues—
OMNES: *R-o-g-u-e-s ...*
JOE: There's rogues in the townland—
MAGUIRE: Nothin' he could do.
MALONE: That's flat porter.

MAGUIRE *and* JOE *break from the propping-each-up position.* MALONE *lands on the floor.*

MALONE: If the second leg had followed the first—

MAGUIRE: The man could do that'd never be bust.

JOE *and* MALONE *now exiting, upstage right and left, respectively.*

JOE: Like a buckin' suck calf and the winds from Siberia ...

MAGUIRE: He'd never be bust—

JOE: And the winds from Siberia ...

MALONE: A treble full multiple odds ... Bettin' on form and breedin' ...

MAGUIRE *alone upstage right – and turning sombre.*

MAGUIRE: The man could do that'd never be bust ...

Scene Eleven

As MARY ANNE *enters upstage left,* MAGUIRE *– facing upstage – is shuffling hesitantly, being sucked towards the kitchen area.*

MARY ANNE: Pigs and cows, Punch and Judy, Punch and Judy, pigs and cows ...

MARY ANNE *advances on* THE MOTHER—

MARY ANNE: I'm getting on in years ... If Mary Anne was settled I'd die in peace ... *Amen* ... The likes of you ... The likes of you ...

MAGUIRE *has arrived.* MARY ANNE *turns her wrath on him—*

MARY ANNE: The likes of you—

MAGUIRE's *response is immediate. He lies down, angle of 45° to the front-stage line, slaps his cap on his face, and – shamelessly infantile – lifts and lets fall his legs, again and again banging the floor: until* MARY ANNE *intervenes, grabs his upraised feet, swivels him towards* THE MOTHER, *lets his feet fall, gets the bag-apron, and pitches it on him, as who should say, 'Now to work, if you're up to it'. That done, she sits down herself, stage left of* THE MOTHER, *removes a shoe, and massages her toes in quiet frenzy.*

MAGUIRE *slides the cap off his face, lifts his head a little, looks at her, muttering and not daring to mutter, garbling the syllables of the word 'mother'.*

MARY ANNE *listens.*

She helps him, as a teacher might, repeating closely, over and over, 'mother' ... 'mother' ... 'mother' ... leading him to clearer articulation, steering him until he gets it right. Finally, the word is spewing from him – and from her. He rises, frothing revolt. MARY ANNE *dons her shoe and joins him, companion-rebel, they've played this out before. She pulls out the drawer, spills everything, tosses the drawer one side. He spreads the bag-apron as table-cloth. And they go to it, taking the objects, rags, dusters, the wire-brush, the bellows, and slamming them on to the bag-apron in rising fury. Next: everything into the maw of the bag.* MARY ANNE *rolls up the bag and slings it to* MAGUIRE – *will he bell the cat?* MAGUIRE *shapes to act, stutters hesitation, crumples, lets the bag fall.*

MARY ANNE, *oozing contempt, gathers it, advances murderously on* THE MOTHER, *raises the loaded bag on high and slams it to the ground directly before* THE MOTHER. *And she exits upstage left.*

Scene Twelve

MAGUIRE *wanders upstage left to lean, head bowed, against the back wall. As if he would vanish into the wall, immobile, he holds there, briefly.*

MAGUIRE *moves, slowly stumbles rather than walks towards the upstage right area, clinging to the back wall.*

Sound-track: 'Lili Marleen', Dietrich version, the recording to suggest the uncertain radio in the farmhouse back of the hills.

Upstage right, MAGUIRE *halts. Turns his attention to the downstage area, vacant attention, wanders downstage. Is drawn to the tabernacle, the gleaming door of the tabernacle. Takes out a tattered handkerchief and polishes the door. Catches his reflection in the door. Studies it – brokenly. Views his face in the door/mirror – as if he has never seen that face before.*

MAGUIRE *breaks from the spectacle. Moves downstage, wiping his mouth with the handkerchief. Halts. Stares into the audience in desolation. Tries to say something. Fails. Moves stage-left to the kitchen-area. Gathers the loaded bag-apron and places it in the drawer. And secures the drawer in its accustomed position, sliding it slowly to. Shutting that door. His big hands against the face of the drawer, his big hands breathing no exit.*

Scene Thirteen

Two centres of simultaneous action.

(1)

MAGUIRE, *buoyant, races to the gate and bellows his (for the moment) delight in being, in sitting on a wooden gate. Over the progress of the* AGNES/MALONE *action (see below), he will produce a sling and fire imaginary missiles at the sky, lie on his back on the top bar of the gate and become the fish in the sunlit pool, straddle the gate and ride flat-out for the winning-post – and win, and, finally, flatten himself upside down on the upstage side of the gate, face on view through the lower bars, legs a V sprouting from the top.*

(2)

As MAGUIRE *takes to the gate,* MALONE *comes on, idles centre-stage, boot scraping mud off his spade. Enter three* YOUNG WOMEN, AGNES *the dominant,* AGNES *seductive and with basket. The three* YOUNG WOMEN *whirl about the space, laughing, teasing* MALONE *without restraint.*

The basket contains a 'rope' made of four black nylons. Availing of it, the supporting YOUNG WOMEN *fashion a shoulder-high fence across which* AGNES, *stage-left, ogles* MALONE, *stage-centre.*

MALONE: Christ, Agnes—
AGNES: How far's it to harvest?
MALONE: Harvest? Christ, Agnes—
AGNES: I know, I know, I know the know—

AGNES *throws a leg across the rope, rides it provocatively.*

AGNES: Play your ace—
YOUNG WOMEN: Jump ... Jump ... Jump ...
AGNES: Jump—
MALONE: Ah Jaysus Agnes—
AGNES: You're soft—
YOUNG WOMEN: Soft ... Soft ... Soft ...

AGNES *clears the rope. She and the* YOUNG WOMEN *cavort about the space, and the rope is given a new position, downstage, waist-high, and on a cross-stage line.*

AGNES *is downstage of the rope. She puts down her basket. Looks at* MALONE. *Moistens her finger, plays it along the bobbling rope, teasily. She lifts the rope over her head, slides it down her back, sits on it, facing* MALONE, *swaying cheekily ...*

AGNES: Oh the men, oh the men—
YOUNG WOMEN: Oh the men, oh the men—
MALONE: She's a flamer!
AGNES: You needn't fear or fret, you needn't—
YOUNG WOMEN: Oh the men, oh the men—
AGNES: You needn't fear or fret, you needn't—
YOUNG WOMEN: Boys oh boys, boys oh boys—

AGNES, *with basket, takes off again, helter-skelter.* MALONE, *growing excited, puts his spade-handle under the rope and the* YOUNG WOMEN *assist in forming a makeshift maypole – around which they spin.* MALONE *is going giddy at the thoughts of daring.*

MALONE: Flat in a furrow, flat in a furrow—
YOUNG WOMEN: Suck, suck-suck-suck ... Sooky suck-suck-suck ...

MALONE: Over on her back!

The maypole dissolves. The YOUNG WOMEN *gambol, race upstage of the gate, return to position themselves stage left, the rope now a little above ankle level.* AGNES *is poised stage-left of the rope.*

MALONE, *in a rush of blood, has meanwhile thrown off his coat, and is slamming the ground belligerently with the flat of his spade.*

AGNES *has a problem. What to do with her basket? She fires it at* MAL-ONE, *who drops his spade, catches the basket, gathers the spade, drops the basket, gathers the basket, shuffles in trepidation.*

AGNES, *uncontainable hoyden, tests the rope for resilience ... We hear a buzzing sound ... Bees? Wasps?* AGNES *jumps in fright, lifts her skirts, delightedly slaps her legs, knees, glowing thighs.*

MALONE *gapes. The crisis passes.* AGNES *resumes her frolic with the rope, pulls it playfully up to crotch-level ...* MALONE *trembles ...*

MALONE: Aisy, Agnes, aisy now—
YOUNG WOMEN: Aisy now, aisy now—
AGNES: Flat in a fur' for the fun of the sun ... Women and men
    for the fun of the sun ...
MALONE: Aisy, Agnes, aisy—
AGNES: Aisy, Agnes, aisy now—
MALONE: No, Agnes, ah Christ Agnes no—

AGNES *swoops. She jumps the rope –* MALONE *drops his spade and the basket. Next* AGNES *grabs his cap and dons it and spins tauntingly about him.*

AGNES: Play your ace—
MALONE: Aisy, Agnes—
AGNES: Play your ace, play your ace—
MALONE: Ah Christ Agnes—
AGNES: Jump, jump—
YOUNG WOMEN: Flat in a fur' ... flat in a fur' ... flat in a fur' ...

MALONE, *moving stage left, flees from* AGNES *but only into the obstacle of the rope. The* YOUNG WOMEN, *manipulating it, sweep him stage centre and into* AGNES's *waiting arms. The* YOUNG WOMEN *bind the pair, and exit echoing snatches from the preceding dialogue.*

AGNES *possesses* MALONE *– almost. The two struggle on the ground.* AGNES *is intent on removing his britches – and comes close to success.*

AGNES: Jump, jump—
MALONE: Mother mercy – no—
AGNES: Jump, jump—
MALONE: Mother – *Mother—*

MALONE *manages to extricate himself, palpitating fright, gathers coat and basket, and rushes off, upstage left.* AGNES *watches him depart.*

AGNES: Oh, you're soft ... Saint ... Saint ... Praties and turnips, worms and frogs ... *Matt Talbot—*

AGNES *gets up. Relaxed. She collects the rope and arranges it about her waist. She steadies* MALONE's *cap on her head.*

AGNES: Oh the men ... Oh the men ...

She collects MALONE's *spade. She studies it, her mood darkens.*

AGNES: Oh the men's the boys—

She exits downstage right, dragging the spade, clatter of the spade a harsh undertow to the rasp of her final comment.

MAGUIRE *has been watching the climax of the* AGNES/MALONE *action from his upside-down position on the gate. He holds there. He clowns, jigging first one foot, then the other.*

PACKY *enters upstage right, a rusty tin can in his possession. He dances slowly along a diagonal which takes him to a position downstage left and close to* THE MOTHER. *He halts. He slowly lifts his right foot, regards it. As that foot rises,* MAGUIRE *moves from his upside-down position on the gate, alters it to hanging, right side up, on the downstage side. He remains suspended there, briefly.*

PACKY *exits downstage left.*

We hear, off, the vicious clatter of the collection-boxes.

MAGUIRE *frees himself from the gate, exits upstage left, at speed.*

Scene Fourteen

The din of the collection-boxes being rattled against each other brings AGNES *on as* MAGUIRE *exits.* AGNES, *in distress, enters upstage left, running; she crosses the space, upstage of the gate, to exit upstage right. She re-enters downstage right and crosses to exit downstage left. Evidently cornered, she re-enters upstage left, runs downstage, halts, and howls her anguish.* MARY ANNE *comes on downstage right, flourishing a collection-box as weapon and barrier.* MAGUIRE, MALONE, PACKY *and* THE SCHOOL-GIRL *arrive. All similarly armed.*

AGNES *is immobilized, mid-space. The pursuers threaten her with the din of collection-box against collection-box.* AGNES *makes a break for it* – PACKY *drives her back.* MALONE *advances, forces a collection-box on her. She accepts it momentarily, drops it, throws it down, rather.* MAGUIRE, *broad as a bishop, puts down his box, advances on the rebel, and forces her to accept the box allocated. She complies.*

Pause. All watch to observe the extent of AGNES's *compliance. She submits, makes the opening move – stiffly raises the box towards her face – in the robotic dance about to commence.*

AGNES's *surrender cues the others. All the layers now move robotically about the space, their limbs – and the boxes – delivered to automaton rhythms. This dance is brief, and finds climax as they stop, and face front, for a photo flash.*

The photo flash and accompanying sound-cue – a reverberating gong – introduces the next phase. The players slide to the ground, lie there, the boxes – however – held upright, like trees, like headstones. And the boxes sway in a lonesome breeze.

THE PRIEST *enters upstage left, takes in the spectacle. He moves towards* THE MOTHER, *and – in the lee of* THE MOTHER – *collects a handful of clay, and wanders among the sleepers blessing them with the clay. The fall of clay on each figure stills the swaying of the tree/headstone.*

THE PRIEST's *progress leaves him downstage right. There he collects a rattle and sounds it to rouse the sleepers.*

The sleepers rise and exit, performing various gestural scores which – echoing the automaton dance – utilize the boxes. Each player has a line which is voiced over and over.

MAGUIRE: Throw another sod on that fire.
AGNES: Watch him.
THE SCHOOL-GIRL: We ought to be finished by the morrow.
MALONE: I see you're breaking your two-year-old.
PACKY: The ace – the last game for me.
MARY ANNE: Play quick, Maguire.

One player – MARY ANNE – fails to join the general exit. Locked in a phrase of her robotic dance, she remains mid-space, stranded.

THE PRIEST *rescues her. He moves in, frees her, takes possession of the box, and exits with her, upstage right.*

Scene Fifteen

THE SCHOOL-GIRL *on, with school-bag and a basin of oats for the hens, making* chooky-chook-chook *noises as she scatters the oats. Gives the audience their share.*

THE SCHOOL-GIRL: Oh to be wise ...

She goes to the kitchen-area, takes from her shoulders the cardigan she's wearing, drapes it about THE MOTHER's *shoulders, whispers to* THE MOTHER, *runs upstage, returns to* THE MOTHER – *gives a kiss to* THE MOTHER. *Upstage again now, and she races for the gate. Takes off her beret and hangs it on the left gate-post. Settles herself upstage side of the gate, peers through the bars, impish.*

THE SCHOOL-GIRL: Oh to be wise ...

She's away again, downstage to the tabernacle: she genuflects to it – scarcely breaking stride, and arrives downstage centre. She's going to say something. She changes her mind. She moistens the tip of each index finger, gravely anoints her closed eyelids, lets her hands fall away, opens her eyes.

She sits now beside the basin. Empties her school-bag of its books. Carefully she makes a pyramid of the books on the flat of the upturned basin, counting in Irish – 'doing her lesson' – the while.

As she starts building the pyramid, MAGUIRE *enters upstage left, rattling coins. He halts, focuses on* THE SCHOOL-GIRL, *and watches her silently from his upstage position. In the same breath,* MARY ANNE *has come on downstage left. She, in turn, focuses on* THE SCHOOL-GIRL. *Eyes on* THE SCHOOL-GIRL. *She drifts to* THE MOTHER, *and, arms about* THE MOTHER, *head resting on* THE MOTHER's *downstage shoulder, watches, watches ...*

The pyramid of books either collapses or is collapsed. And THE SCHOOL-GIRL *becomes a barking terrier, picks up her school-bag, and runs off upstage right, working a repose of her counting-in-Irish verbal score.*

Scene Sixteen

MAGUIRE *advances downstage, halts stage right of* THE MOTHER. *He's rattling coins, glancing at intervals into the cup of his joined hands.* MARY ANNE *is by* THE MOTHER, *as indicated above.* MAGUIRE *gives up on the coins. The atmosphere is comfortless.*

MAGUIRE: What was I doing?
MARY ANNE: Where was I looking?
MAGUIRE: Young women and men—
MARY ANNE: Men and women – I might have joined them—
MAGUIRE: I remember a night we walked through the moon—
MARY ANNE: A moon o' Donaghmoyne —
MAGUIRE: The four of us—
MARY ANNE: Seekin' adventure—
MAGUIRE: It was mid-summer—
MARY ANNE: Summer—

MAGUIRE *resumes rattling the coins – but mime, this time, soundless. He hums morosely. And* MALONE, *drink taken and exhibiting that belligerence, comes on, upstage right, driving* PACKY *before him with the aid of an ash-plant.* PACKY *is cradling an ass-collar. Framed in the collar is a turnip-head (carved à la Hallowe'en), the head impaled on a short stick. The effect should be of a Voodoo-child, ambiguous, mocking.*

The entrance of the pair is raucous.

MALONE: Maguire ... Maguire ... Maguire, you're wrong ... You're wrong about that thing I was telling you ... Poor Paddy Maguire ... The bridge is too narrow ... the bridge is too narrow, Maguire ...

MARY ANNE's *response to the incursion is to pick up a boot downstage right and commence cleaning it, obsessively, with a corner of her apron.*

PACKY, *orchestrated by* MALONE, *is circling* MAGUIRE, *holding up the turnip-child, baiting* MAGUIRE *with the picture. And* MALONE *jeers—*

MALONE: And thirty-five could take the sparrow's bow!

MAGUIRE *agrees to view this dubious offering, perhaps even make an offering in response – there's a mug attached to the collar, evidently a receptacle for coins. As* MAGUIRE *looks at the turnip-child,* PACKY – *manipulating the stick – slowly turns the head to meet* MAGUIRE's *look. Pause ...* MAGUIRE *drops his coins in the mug.* MALONE *crows triumph—*

MALONE: And you'll have all the luck ... You'll have all the luck!

Bruised, MAGUIRE *wanders to an upstage-right position, again seeks shelter against the back wall – as* MALONE *and* PACKY *sweep on in search of fresh victims.* MARY ANNE *is an obvious mark.* MALONE *loosing drover-cries, the pair descend on her. She doesn't wait to present a target but, relinquishing her makeshift chore (the boot-cleaning), exits at speed, upstage left,* MALONE *and* PACKY *in vociferous pursuit.*

Scene Seventeen

Enter two YOUNG WOMEN *wearing black head-scarves and black aprons. They march. One carries a towel. The first briskly removes the cardigan from* THE MOTHER, *takes the bucket (downstage left), and sloshes water over the 'corpse'. The second – same brisk idiom – dries off*

THE MOTHER. *Then, together, they drape a white sheet over* THE MOTHER, *and look around for* – MAGUIRE. *They spot him upstage left, sheltering by the wall. Resolutely, they march to that point, and commandeer him. He resists, shouting in Irish—*

MAGUIRE: Ná bac léi ... Ná bac léi ...

Nevertheless, they drag him to THE MOTHER, *drag him backwards across the space and position him beside the sheeted corpse.*

And the two YOUNG WOMEN *exit, in lockstep.*

Scene Eighteen

MAGUIRE *standing with his back to the sheeted* MOTHER. *He stretches out a hand. Touches the sheet. A spasm of fright through him. He rushes away from* THE MOTHER *and into a fit of pegging stones at the back wall, dodging their ricochet.*

That passes. Centre-stage, he takes off his cap. Blesses himself. Moves again towards THE MOTHER. *He takes the sheet and drags it away so that the face is exposed. Again he moves back, pauses centre-stage, flings his cap over the gate and away.*

He returns to THE MOTHER. *He must kiss the corpse. He circles. He moves in. He wavers. He closes. Crying like an animal, he kisses* THE MOTHER.

Again he breaks away. Rushes to the gate. Whistles for his dog. There's a surge of animal noises, and four (or more) of the players come on, upstage right and left, in animal guise. They gather upstage of the gate, battering at its bars, and the animal sounds rise to a din.

MAGUIRE – *a bucket in his clutches – stumbles towards the gate, opens the gate. The animals pour through, knocking him over, rushing over him and past him to exit variously.*

Scene Nineteen

MAGUIRE – *gathering the bucket, holding it close – scrambles upstage, humps down by the right gate-post.*

MAGUIRE: Dragged ... Dragged ... Dragged home a drunken man on a winter's night ... No man ... Helped a poor woman whose cow died on her ... No man ... Heard the young people playing on the railway stile, wished them happiness ... No man ... No man, begrudged no man his share ... The spade, the spade, Joe, don't forget – ... Eileen ... Eileen ... Eileen. Eileen, Eileen, Eileen – who was Eileen? She was a daisy ... Joe, don't forget to hide the spade ... The fields is white ... Jesus, Mary, and Joseph, pray for us now and at the hour ... Hail Holy Queen, Mother o' Mercy ...

Scene Twenty

THE PRIEST, MARY ANNE, AGNES, THE SCHOOL-GIRL, *and* PACKY,

enter from various points. THE PRIEST *carries his missal,* THE SCHOOL-GIRL *a lighted candle.* MALONE *brings* MAGUIRE's *overcoat and spade. He spreads the overcoat centre-stage and rests the spade on it.*

AGNES *has brought a green-leaved branch: she drops it on the overcoat.* PACKY *has brought his dented tin can: that also goes on to the overcoat. And* MARY ANNE *– in possession of* MAGUIRE's *cap – throws that on to the pile.*

THE PRIEST *rouses* MAGUIRE *by the gate-post. The two shake hands.* THE PRIEST *indicates the overcoat, the pile of objects.* MAGUIRE *goes to that point. To choose. He takes the overcoat. Puts it half on, and moves downstage right.*

MALONE, MARY ANNE, AGNES *and* PACKY *recover spade, cap, branch, and tin can, respectively.*

THE PRIEST, *by the gate, is poised to lead the departure procession.*

MAGUIRE *moves centre-stage.* MALONE *shuffles forward, shakes* MAGUIRE's *hand, whispers briefly, goes upstage to wait behind* THE PRIEST. PACKY *– his tin can held like an offering – goes to* MAGUIRE. MAGUIRE *looks away.* PACKY *joins the line forming upstage.* AGNES *advances, holding her branch. She and* MAGUIRE *look at each other.* MAGUIRE *touches a leaf of the branch.* AGNES *joins the upstage line.* MARY ANNE *goes to* MAGUIRE, MARY ANNE *kneading his cap, bleakly. She doesn't look at* MAGUIRE. *His look for her is sidelong, constrained.* MARY ANNE *joins the upstage line.*

THE PRIEST *leads the procession through the gate and off, upstage left.* THE SCHOOL-GIRL, *with lighted candle, is left. She moves quickly to close the gate, stubbing the candle in the same motion, and half-running off to catch up with the others. Close to the exit-point, she stops – as if remembering – and gives a brief backward glance to* MAGUIRE. *Then she exits freely.*

Scene Twenty-One

MAGUIRE *alone in weakening light. He moves about the space with the awkward grace of an animal nosing about for a clean place to die. His foot paws the ground searchingly – here, there, elsewhere. Soon enough he's satisfied – or he abandons the search. He lies down, gives himself to the ground.* MAGUIRE *is still.*

Finis

The Gallant John-Joe
for Ger

Design

Mangle upstage right, chair beside it ... story-telling chair stage left ... a shelf on the mangle provides room for a bottle of pills and two bottles of medicine ... hanging from above, just off centre, a Chinese lantern, lit. Dirty brown lino defines the playing area.

Prologue

(Fade-up from black. JOHN-JOE *is standing centre, gulping from large medicine bottle.)*

So I'm lugged off to the hospital, first time in me life I entered the like and for why? I've bumps on me nuts, if ye don't mind, and them could finish ye. I told the doctor – Leave them, fuck them, pawn them for tuppence-halfpenny, but between him and Jacinta I was drove to it. So there I am lyin' on a wheelbarrow o' some description in a dark room, ready to be made a negative of, nothing on me but a class of a torn shift, not enough in it to dust a fiddle. In comes this Paki or Madigascar or how's your mother, and next he has some invention of a Lazarus beam on me nuts and bolts and they're coming up on a screen he can see but I can't. 'I'm sorry it's taking so long,' says he, after an hour or two. 'It's for the good of the outpatient.' Eventually, I'm let go. 'You will be informed in time to come of the course of events,' says he, and disappears, melted into a tiled wall – the place was fuckin' full of them, lick of the tar-brush, every breed y'ever saw barrin' the Eskimo, and they probably had them below in the basement beside the furnace. Tuk home by ambulance, broke down twice in the way, you're only a number in the hands of a pack from the other side of the globe – what's left of it.

(Takes another slug from the bottle ... goes to the mangle, sits, and, working the wheel of the mangle – it transforms to hurdy-gurdy – he sings 'The Gallant John-Joe'.)

In the month of November 'twas a wild stormy day / I shut the front door and to town made me way / I met with a young man on the road I did go / And he told me the news of the death of John-Joe ... He led Cavan to victory on a glorious day / In the Polo Grounds Final when Kerry gave way / In Croke Park the next year when our boys bet Mayo / Once again they were led by the gallant John-Joe ... In each corner of Breiffne there's sorrow and pain / Such a great-hearted sportsman we'll ne'er see again / Grand players may come and grand players may go / But we'll ne'er find the likes of the gallant John-Joe ...

Scene One

(He takes up the pills, decides against ... goes for the small bottle of medicine, has a slug ... grimaces and murmurings of unease ... small bottle back to its positions on the mangle ... now he walks to the story-chair, hiking trousers as he goes, massaging his lumbar region, halts.)

Th'oul lumbar's a hoor. Th'oul lumbar.

(Moves centre.)

I have this daughter – Jacinta – she's carrying a child, a chirpaun. A lock of arguments risin' on the head of that chirpaun. I do keep askin' wan question – first question anyone'd ask – only she flings it back at me. 'Why bother asking,' says she, 'when you've already decided you know the answer?' The contraptious bitch! 'I'll keep asking,' says I, 'till I find out what I've a right to know. You're my daughter, I'm that chirpaun's grandfather. I'm entitled to know who – when – and where the father's to be found – if to be found. I've an obligation to know where that chirpaun originated.' Is she listenin'? Enough to pick up me word – *obligation*. 'The chirpaun and meself,' says she, 'we've our obligations too.'

'And what might they be?' says I. 'Oh,' says she, 'obligations to take it easy, to prepare for an event. Obligations to keep in touch with the father, as seems right and proper.' 'You're in touch with the father then?' says I. 'To be sure I am,' says she. 'How in touch?' says I. 'All kinds of ways of keepin' in touch,' says she, 'carrier pigeon, smoke signals, notes left under stones. But the best of all is telepathy – where, without moving a finger, you communicate just by thinking. That's the quickest and the simplest.' 'What kind of a hammer-head do you take me for?' says I. 'Carrier pigeons, smoke signals, telepathy, tele-fuckin-pathy?' 'Animals does it,' says she, 'all the time.' And she's gone for a walk.

(He shifts from standing position to sitting on the story-chair.)

I know the bastard done it. The Chinee what runs the chipper below. God forgive me, wasn't I the one encouraged her to take the job with him. I know it was him, didn't I walk her to the chipper the first day she clocked in. He couldn't wait, seen it with me own two eyes, couldn't wait to get her upstairs or backstairs or wherever he deep-fries his trombone. 'Match the genes', Boss-Man is advisin', 'DMA, they can do that nowadays.' 'Thanks, Lord Know-All,' says I to meself. 'Match the genes!' he's still at it. 'The genes is matched,' says I, 'too fuckin' well-matched.' ... Boss-Man. The brave Boss-Man. We used to go fishin'. The little bit he knows about anglin', I learned him. 'Very well to do', as they say around here. Maynin' money streamin' out of orifices, not to mention the lawdidawdy engineer accent. Claims he travelled most of the known world. Picked up his trade coaxin' sweet oil from the desert sands near Da-Rann. A non-stop sermonizer. In here last week, first thing he wants to know – 'You taking your medication, Concannon?' 'What about the bastardin' side-effects?' says I. 'Name them.' 'Main side-effect is they cripple you,' says I. 'How's Jacinta?' says he. 'Outa the chipper,' says I. 'And I thought the chipper'd be the makings of her.' 'Instead of which it's the makings of something else,' says I. 'Look,' says I, 'It's not her carrying a chirpaun I mind. Not but I'd take a crucifix to whatever cunt done it. It's not that ... it's ... Listen – am I to spend the last years of me days watchin' – puttin' up with – the child of a daughter of mine walking this town like ... Like the great-grandson of some pig-tailed Confucius you'd swim into a lake to get out of the way of? ... Could she not let it be one of her own? Instead of leavin' me standin' here, baw-ways, tongue in me mouth dry as a stick, all on the head of the sure promise of a squintin' face yellow at the window?' ... You might as well be talkin' to a chest of drawers. 'John-Joe,' I'm told, 'You must get out and about. You must circulate. Blood circulates. Air circulates. Fester you're finished. Next stop The Great Empty Quarter.' And out the door in smoke. 'Blood circulates.' Damn wonder he didn't take me pulse – like he takes Jacinta's every time he gets the chance ... Meantime, I'm getting no further. Neither hide nor hair of a father, the town gabblin' of nothing else. Any attempt I make to find out, off she floats into the but-termilk blue of the high above. But I wasn't giving in. Back I went to her ladyship again. 'Was it The Chinee?' She's sittin' there, ear-phones stuck to her lugs and the Sony Talkman pipin' music to the wee hero within. 'Did ye hear me question, daugh-ter?' 'I was countin' sheep, put it by me again, please.' 'Was it The Chinee?' Know what she does? Pulls up the blouse, slaps the ear-phones to the swell of her belly – she'll find out direct from the chirpaun if it was The Chinee. 'Hey, you in there, was it The Chinee?' says she. Listens. 'Sorry, didn't catch that.' Explains to me His Lordship's only learnin' to put words together and repeats the question. 'Was it The Chinee?' Listens again. And reports back the big news – impident grin on her. 'Chirpaun's response is as follows: that'll all be known when the waters break and flow under the bridge and down the Swanny-O.' The Hayro has spoken from her far within – if I ask another question he'll likely give me the Campdown Races dee-di doo-dah-day. Fearsome how she can keep the gob shut once she decides it's government policy. So there I am, left lyin' in rigmarole. But I knows me next step.

Scene Two

(*He rises, moves to stage right ...*)

There's this Hitmatist operatin' below in the town – they're goin' to him in processions, comin' away from the place dancin'. The New Druid, bejazus!

(*Takes out newspaper cutting, reads.*)

'Fully qualified Hypnotherapeutic Treatment for maladies of all varieties including Cancer, Brain Tumours, Tiredness, Exhaustion, Panneumatic Upsets, Weight Addition or Weight Loss and Larger Business Success. Miracle Cure-Line – nought four one, treble seven, double three two. Agoraphobics welcome.'

(*Puts cutting away.*)

Anyways, I'll give it a try, I decides. Might ease the hurt mind the bit. And I lands in there. White mansion he has with long-legged young ones waltzing around the shiny corridors. And they've fifty quid outa me pocket before they've the coat off me back.

(Coat off, puts it on story chair.)

Plus, I'm being bombardeered with music outa the walls and lights – there's lights, coloured and bright and dark you'd never imagine – all introduced by The Hitmatist himself from a lap-top gazebo throbbin' on his knees. And when he has me nicely light in the head, he advances on me and lowers me onto one of them sofas with no end to one end of it, equipped with a pedal – and his foot's on the pedal – that'll shift you up, down, and sideways in the same commotion.

(Moves chair up-centre, sits.)

So there I am, prostate – bamboozled by the chair-o-plane cir-cus – I haven't the strength to pull a herring off a tongs. And he's just standing there – starin' me – not a word outa him. 'Christ,' says I to meself, 'if it goes on like this, I'll be a candidate for Extreme Unction.' But now he's beside me. A very quiet voice. 'Mr Concannon – welcome – Dallan Devine.' 'I don't know what to say,' says I. 'Talk when you're ready,' says he. And it's conve-nient for him to start massagin' me skull – fingers like a con-certina. 'We must encourage the blood to attend to our needs, Mr Concannon,' he's saying, 'And we, in turn, must attend to the needs of the restless blood.' Meantime, I'm afloat on the Red Sea! 'I have this daughter,' says I, 'Jacinta.' And I takes out the photo of Jacinta I bears regular on me person and I gives it to him. And bejazus he's looking at her – the arrival of the Promised Land! Like she was passin' into his corpuscles! 'Handsome young woman,' says he. I think I seen a lot of what was to come in that particular remark. 'She's carrying a child,' says I, 'I know who done it.' 'You know the father and you saw it coming but were powerless to intervene. Now you want to shoot him and live happily ever after. Likely wasn't the one you think.' 'Who was it then?' says I. 'Seldom is,' says he, and he eye-ballin' me like I was deaf. 'Seldom is!' says I, 'Where's that landin' me on the issue of paternity? I'd be better off at home takin' me medication.' But before I depart, says I to meself, I'll draw blood, I'll leave me mark on some section of this performer's anatomy. So I sits up and says I – 'Dallan Devine – ye made that name up, ye get ye!' 'Correct, Mr Concannon,' says he, 'I made it up.' 'I had you taped,' says I. 'And why'd a man the like of you go to the bother of making up his name now?' 'Simply answered,' says he. 'But first bear in mind that we all – all – make up our names in some fashion or other. Furthermore, my choice of name, Dallan Devine, and I can vouch for this, gives powerful assurance to the patient in need of assurance, proven sustenance to the troubled approaching The Unapproachable.' And the farrango he comes out with – he didn't stop for ten minutes. On and on he goes like some class of a one-man Oul Moore's Almanack or your boyo, Nostring-damus, spewin' prophecies. I just sat there in me spin – glaucoma'd. It was on me tongue to throw in – 'Sorry, Professor, I don't know Esperantine' – but I let it pass. Next thing –

(*He rises, and stands centre-stage.*)

– don't I get terrible upset and I hears meself – 'What'd a man be

gettin' outa bed in the mornin' for?' says I to him, 'There's a cra-
dle in the corner and a chirpaun whingin'. Turn your back,
they're grown childher. Nod – they're on top of other, goats of
the field. Another nod, you're grey hairs. Fart – and you're
scutch-grass, poor man's corner of the bone-yard. Tell me, Mr
Hitmatist, what's that about? What's that all about?' 'It's about
affliction, Mr Concannon,' says he, 'Your affliction.' And then
the whore went for me. 'Sexually active?' says he. 'Pardon?' says
I. 'Are you sexually active?' 'Sure, amn't I half crippled,' says I,
'It's a short tippin'-season for lots, you know.' 'Age?' 'What age
are you?' says I. 'Widower?' 'That's right.' 'How long?' 'This six-
teen year.' 'Any relationships formed or forming with another
female or females since your wife's demise?' 'No,' says I, 'Is that
all right?' 'You tell me, Mr Concannon,' says he, 'I have in mind
stress, proximity, one-parent intimacies.' 'Repeat that,' says I.
'One-parent intimacies,' says he, 'That dusk.' Well, I nearly
fuckin' went for him. I could hear the ticker going like a
thresher. Went for me coat instead – started to put it on – when
Sweet Christ sweatin' on the cross, didn't I take a terrible turn!
It's like the floor goes on fire –

*(He takes his coat, flings it on the floor, commences trampling it, stomping
out the imaginary flames.)*

– and I'm tramplin' with me overcoat tryin' to quench the blaze.
But the blaze keeps comin' – I'm leaves for the burning! Then
there's a firm hand on me shoulder and a delicate whisper in me
ear. And the fit stops. 'Sit down, Mr Concannon,' says he. And I
did.

(He sits on the mangle-chair, holding coat.)

'Could I have that picture of Jacinta back?' says I. 'Certainly, Mr Concannon,' says he. 'Thanks,' says I. I was that weak I couldn't push a cat off a stool. 'Reason I'm coming to see you is I get upset about lots of things,' says I. 'Don't pass no remarks on me, Dallan Devine. You said unapproachable. What's that mean in decent language?' 'That on which you dare not lay your hand,' says he. 'Great pleasure, Mr Concannon. Melanie will show you out.'

Scene Three

(*He sits ... mutters under his breath the first verse of the ballad ... then to the mangle, settles there, works the wheel, and sings that verse ...*)

In the month of November 'twas a wild stormy day / I shut the front door and to town made me way / I met with a young man on the road I did go / And he told me the news of the death of John-Joe ...

(*Rises from chair and moves into the choreography of taking a free kick: drying ball on clothing ... placing ball in best position ... targeting goalposts ... stepping back, drying boot on 'sock' ... now the run-up and kick ...*)

Doubt ye boy! *Thar an treasnán!*

(*He beams at the posts, then goes back to the mangle, settles there, works the handle, sings ...*)

Grand players may come and grand players may go / But we'll not find the likes of the gallant John-Joe ...

(He studies the mangle.)

She's an heirloom. I could get a mint for her in any of them museums is to be found in every old hayshed these days. A mint. Only, there's some things you don't let go of. Anyways, what'd I be doing with a fortune in me fist? No pockets in the habit is what I was always told. No, nor buttons on the shroud.

(He has found time during the above speech to clean the mangle with a rag ... for climax, he kisses it ... Sings:)

Sleep, o, babe, for the red bee hums the silent twilight's fall / Aoibheall from the grey rock comes to wrap the world in thrall / A leanbhan, o, me child, me joy, me love and heart's desire / The cricket sings you lullaby beside the dying fire ...

(Ceremonially, he gives the mangle a final kiss.)

Mary's song. She had it outa Donegal somewhere. I could never rightly tell what came over that woman of mine.

(He sits on the mangle chair.)

She was a young Miss Ireland – broke hearts like they were kipeens, kipeens you'd throw on the fire. Then she falls in with John-Joe Concannon. I flung a halter on her, a job, but I done it. We get shackled, and then what happens? She'd Rose, Rita, and Jacinta all in a rush – then lay down and gave up. God rest her soul, I mind her as well as bread. Not a day passes but I see her lookin' out that kitchen window. Daughters and mothers, mothers and daughters. Mostly mystery is the way I'd describe them.

Mystery mostly. Maybe meant to be that way. So's they can slap more spells on us. They're a fearsome bag of spells, the female women. Fearsome. But coming back to the barbed-wire question of paternities, our oul friend DMA –

(*He rises and moves to centre-stage.*)

– certain steps were taken by me to deal with the hot favourite – Mr Lee Chang Woo – of which more anon in the soon to be. Grand! I arrives back in the house with a few bags of chips. There she is, knitting another gansy for the wee hero. Gave her one of the bags. 'Thought I'd take a ramble down to the chipper,' says I, 'stir the pot a bit. Had a few words with your former employer, The Chinee in his Chef's Hat. Spots me, and all of a sudden he's woeful busy. "Scuse me," says I, and I lugged him out to the back-yard. You should have seen the jandied puss of him, turning the colour of Indian meal gone mildewed – if you'd call that a colour. I spots Mrs The Chinee taking a gander from the window above. Well, I smigged him the twice. Then I milled him with the boot – by which time he's pumpin' the red stuff. Left him lying on top of the fish-boxes, a handy dose of quiet in him. Looked up and Herself waves me inside. She gave me a full cod-and-chips on the house – the giving hand. She's a dowser!' 'Did she not give you the run of the parlour?' says me daughter. 'I had other preoccupations,' says I. 'The belly loaded, I'm thinking I'm not done with him yet, boy! Had a look. Not in the yard. Seems he crawls his way from the fish-boxes to lick his contusions in the bed above. Which is where I interrogate him. Told me – what I knew – about inveigling you free of your britches, and tastes so honey he can't help himself ever after. But one slippery latchicoe. On me way out denies everything. Sez he only made it up to smoother me down.'

(Firming himself centre, king of all he surveys.)

'Well, I went back – took him by the thrapple. Name, says I, name the colour, exact colour of Jacinta's hair – I'm referring to the pubic foliage. Name it, says I, name it, ye clem ye, sure as saucers there's an eye in your head knows it. What does he do? Starts to stutter and froth. So I fired him there. Watch this space, says I, for further severe castringations as required.' ... Jacinta sitting there. Only now she's gone all quiet on me. Heinous quiet. 'Me body's me own,' says she. 'Body me own, pubic foliage me own. I'm talking about a person, a daughter, me, standing in front of you. A one you can't see, a one you'll never see. Cos all you can see is your own grip. Melt the grip or there'll be nothing to grip. I'm outa here. I'll be wherever I land. You'll have the bothawn here to yourself. John-Joe Concannon licking the walls and the fire out.' ... This is my Jacinta talking. Her back to me, voice so low you have to stretch to hear her. 'I'm a person.' Last thing she says. 'I'm a person.' And the swish of her out the door.

(Turbulent pause.)

It wasn't me mentioned pubic foliage! That's her term the first day. Some of them radio phones-ins. Pubic foliage! The tongues of women, soft as church music, then she roars into a tear – Take your paws offa me! ... Wasn't it exactly on her behalf – no one else's – that I confronts that kinky-eyed Romeo below, gives her me account, and I'm in the dock for a numbered inmate in the House of Pariahs! She didn't accuse The Chinee! – the innocent malefactor – may his soul turn into a Peking duck and paddle the

sinks of Hell forever! If you want the heart-scald have ten daughters. They'll turn on you – the viper tooth and serve you right!
You're a conscript Armenian on your way to Armageddon and
the liquid slopes of Golgotha!

(*He simmers momentarily on those liquid slopes.*)

All right, says I to meself. What's the butt of the row here? Your
valubles, me lady, your valubles, is my answer to that question.
Where your valubles is put on offer. There's responsibilities, you
know. And where them particular valubles is concerned, I'm not
turning me back on what's mine to guard and protect. Who'd
thank me? Johnny Magorey? Fine. Dance while you're limber –
but down the lane I'm the one blamed for not taking charge and
the harm done. Jacinta, how'd this bargin' start? ... I'm talking to
meself. I gave up. Went for a walk down by the lake, thanking
God it's not Christmas. 'Cos the lakes around hereabouts in the
Christmas season – whatever comes over them – is peculiar
inviting. You could put watch-towers around the same lakes and
still not hold back them what hears the call. That's a known fact.

Scene Four

(*He sits on the story-chair, takes out the photo of Jacinta, studies it.*)

There was two. Now there's one. On your owneeoh ...

(*Puts photo away.*)

I fell into a steep decline. Took to the bed mostly. Did you ever hear of an isolated ward? Ever hear of an isolated kitchen? It has four walls and a ceiling and they're looking at you. Looking at you, keeping the closest eye, John-Joe Concannon, for the knuckles of a month. Ate nothing. 'If I can taste nothing,' says I, 'nothing'll pass these lips.' Her Ladyship'd surface – at unforecastable intervals – a lassie unwilling to recognize me mortal existence. My Jacinta. Outa nowhere, I'm one of them stateless persons marooned in some border purgatory. Grand! Middle of the second week her mouth opens. 'If you're not in the humour of eating a pick, I'm getting the doctor.' The which she does. Baldy Hippocrates. Told him I was in swithers and swives about the paternity question. He presents me a bottle, sez he'll speak with Jacinta. 'Good luck,' says I. He sloothers off. Am I left in quiet? O, no. Baldy Hippocrates passes the word. There's a hammering on the door. I sit tight. Hammering continues. I admits the caller, the brave Boss-Man. Closes the door and – if I might be permitted ...

(He rises and moves to centre.)

– to interrupt meself here – a morsel of wisdom and for free. Don't – when you're bleeding like a stuck pig – don't be looking for friends to staunch the flow. Old friends especially. And the one particular old friend – keep an eye on that party! Meaning? Meaning this. The one particular old friend – at your shoulder for years – has a hidden agenda. That's right, a hidden agenda. Door-banger Boss-Man and uninvited guest now standing right fornenst me. He was all right, not the worst for a pile of years. Only lately – Jacinta springin' into her bosom – another element comes into play. Doesn't he turn into a Counsellor – a Welfare

Officer – glory be to God – with an expandin' exponential invest-ment in my daughter's well-being. 'What are you doing in here? Get out, John-Joe,' says he. 'Don't be sitting cooped up in a room with Jacinta. Not healthy.' Damn well I knew what he was impli-cating. 'Why's it not healthy?' says I, putting it right up to his smig. Sidesteps that one – develops a sudden interest in the infested remains of the handball alley, last used nineteen and thirty-two, year of the Eucharistic Congress. 'Holiday is what you need, Concannon, I'll pay for it.' And he'll keep an eye on Jacinta when I'm gone. O, yes, I'm sure. Feel her pulse at hourly intervals. Or Jacinta should take off – he'll pay for everything – she needs to stretch her legs, get a bit of sun on her pelt. 'Tell you what,' says I. 'Why don't you send Jacinta and me on a holi-day – the Singin' Canaries – and you come with us as a chaperon and health adviser of a general nature?' He gives me a look. 'I take that kind of talk amiss, Concannon,' says he. And the nose skewways, outa joint, retreats from the field! 'Fine,' says I, 'fine.' Now he knows I knows his rabid inclinings.

(*Swirl of silence ... followed by spasm of action. He moves into football choreography of blocking down an opponent's delivery ... kicked by an opponent ... outstretched hands first right, then left ... and reprise ...*)

John-Joe Reilly. He had a way – a method – because, by Christ, there was method in it – a way of blocking down a ball, that had to do with timing – timing – and the swoop – done – QED – Good-night, Joe Doyle! Commandant John-Joe Reilly – greatest centre-half of the modern era – Millennium All-Star and Prince of The Immortals ...

(*He sings.*)

Grand players may come and grand players may go / But we'll not find the likes of the gallant John-Joe ...

(*Goes to the mangle, gets large medicine bottle, takes a slug from it – which provokes the usual grimaces and mutterings of distaste ... then back to centre and he slides into reflective vein.*)

There was a magazine in the long ago, about that size magazine ...

(*Indicates dimensions.*)

... You'd see it at school – was called *The Far East* ... And what was that magazine attempting to propagate? The conversion – if you don't mind – of the heathen hordes along the Yangtse River. Every month it'd come. Open it up. The pictures in it. There they are looking out at you. The faces of them heathen hordes asking for to be baptized on the banks of the Yangtse River. Glory be to Christ – *The Far East* ...

Scene Five

(*Returns bottle to mangle, leans on the mangle.*)

Anyways, a few weeks flitters by. Four walls and one ceiling watching their Prisoner of Zenda. Daughter Jacinta dreeping resentments. Baldy Hippocrates with his quack ministrations. One day worse nor another. But even in the isolated kitchen you'll always have, thanks be to God, some form of a distraction. I looks up for want of anything better to do. Who's in the doorway, in the kitchen, settling himself comfortable, only The Hitmatist. 'What in Christ's name are you doing here?' says I. 'Jacinta invited me,' I'm informed. And she comes down from above and confirms these very interesting tidings. 'Why wouldn't I invite him,' says she, 'a social celebrity. I'm aiming to extend me education.' 'Is he going to hear your Confession?' I ask her. That's laughed off – and the visit passes harmless enough. Only is it? Shape of the bag's one thing. What comes out of the bag is another. When they're gone outa that, it hits me. How did I not see it coming?

(*He crosses to centre.*)

Mr Hitmatist! First, I shows him the picture of Jacinta – and I've a job to get it back off him, as you might remember. Next, he lands up here in the house – on one of his corpulent works of mercy, moryah! That's number two. What's them manoeuvres the commencement of? Just this. The next day Boss-Man walks in with the story that me daughter is now a client of The Hitmatist – free treatment for needy cases if you don't mind. And she's wearing a path to his door. And what's more, according to me informant, there's dozens of pictures of Jacinta – raunchy, Concannon, raunchy – lining a curved corridor of the mansion. 'Naked?' says I. 'No, but lingeries – as far as is known,' says Boss-Man and him upright with palpitations on the head of his own credentials. 'Where'd you hear that?' says I. 'Whole town has it, John-Joe,' says he. 'We're not speaking of rumour here.' 'Grand,' says I, 'and if they're all as excited as you are with the smell of it, look for widespread convulsions before night.' And threw him out. And sat down. And reflected.

(*He sits on the story-chair.*)

No fool like an old fool. That was well said the first day whoever came out with it. No fool like the old fool. Her below mountin' him – that I'm going to – to get rid of stress – that she's causing to begin with – and that he, she, the two of them, is now magnifying like there was no tomorrow! It's like a riddle you couldn't make up – not if you had the head of Homer. I must be blind as Sinbad tied to the mast and turning salt. Straight off I thought, I'll go down to Mr Dallan Devine, invade the premises, and beat the bastard into an ointment. Then I thought – No, John-Joe, no. That's putting him in the right. Go to your legal adviser and take the cocksman to court for interfering with a female client of tender years. But then I thought – No, no, no. Go down to the mansion, march in and collect th'evidence. The whole clutch of them scandalous pictures. Ah, but then says I to meself – John-Joe, inspect those pictures you'll lose the run of yourself, you won't be responsible! You're only fresh from risking life and limb on the Asiatic front! March down to your solicitor – it comes back to that. And I'm on me way out the door when in strolls Jacinta, The Hitmatist's new friend and old acquaintance. 'How's Mr Devine?' says I. 'He'll last till midnight anyways,' says she – not holding back from proffering prevarications. 'I'd leave now, Jacinta,' says I. 'Pack your duds, there's the door.' 'Boss-Man's calling you demented,' says she. 'I must be blind as Sinbad tied to the mast and turning salt,' says I. I was bulling. Bulling! I ask her the second time to leave. 'There's the door,' says I. She's not even listening. She's taking it easy. Strolling the kitchen, exercising herself, gentle like, you're looking at a dove or a doe. The belly. Feeling the wee hero indoors. Is she out of her skull? Has he her on drugs below? So she sits. Eyes me. And drops her small bombshell. 'Hitmatist, Pa, is a fraud,' says she. 'You knows that. I knows it. So on to other matters of more concern.' Well, there's no telling anything until it shows the noggin above the parapet. So The Hitmatist is out of the equation! Thanks be to Jazus, *Slán beo*, Dallan Devine! Next she sidles over and parks beside me. 'I was talking to your man, Curley, used to work with you in the Creamery beyond in Roscommon,' says she. 'That's not today nor yesterday,' says I. 'He told me all about the row,' says she. 'What was done to you because you were different. John-Joe Concannon had vision but they couldn't rise to it,' Curley kept saying. 'Jumps ahead of the time you were. The way he saw it you were the light was smothered. Vexed me to the gut listening to him, the abuse you took from that pack. I cried for two hours after,' says she. And gives me a hug. 'You need minding, Pa,' says she, 'and you'll get it. There's nobody going nowhere outa this place. Minding each other is our business and we'll meet that obligation.'

(*He sighs, ample sigh.*)

Jacinta! ... I just sat there, didn't know what to say or do. She gives me another hug and I starts cryin'. Then she makes a sup of tea and we starts gostering the way we used to before the woes of time tethered me on hasky ground. 'Mind the time you had the pointer and retriever,' says she. 'Aye,' says I, 'Bran – and Smokey – with the gammy leg.' And there she is – racin' around the place, pretending she's Bran and Smokey like she used to when she was knee-high to a grasshopper. And laughing and talking about those days, and Uncle Sha and Mickey The Pound. 'Poor Uncle Sha. What age would he be now?' says she. 'Topping the ninety,' says I. 'Walked into a lake in the middle of the night.

Wanted to see how deep it was, I suppose!'

(*He laughs happily.*)

Like old times it was, old times and the hay saved. I sat back. If I was a Siamese I'd have purred ... Jacinta starts up an old jingle we used to warble in them times. 'Must be years since we gave it a lash, Pa,' says she. 'Sinbad the Sailor,' says she. 'And Binbad the Bailer,' says I. And Dinbad the Dailer. And Finbad the Failer. And Hinbad the Hailer. And Jinbad the Jailer. And Kinbad the Kailer. And Minbad the Mailer. And Ninbad the Nailer ... Listen to me, I was damn near the most contented man in The Ring of Ireland. Damn near. Damn near. Sometimes I imagine them words written on me birth certificate. John-Joe damn near Concannon. Aye ... Name the man dipped his wick. The procreator. It was there in me cranium, stinging away ... Never mind. Truth'll out ...

(*He rises, crosses to the mangle, works the wheel, and sings.*)

He led Cavan to victory on a glorious day / In the Polo Grounds Final when Kerry gave way / The next year in Croke Park when our boys bet Mayo / Once again they were led by the Gallant John-Joe ...

(*Spins into gestural score of showing the ball to an opponent, then whipping it away – impudent tease ... and reprise of that ...*)

And watch him – view him – defer to that man – showing opponents the ball – giving them a dekko – 'Here, look, it's a football' – then jooks back, shows it again to the unfortunate stooge now prostate in the muck – and elegant – elegant, Ladies and Gentlemen – delivers to Higgins on the forty or Tighe on the wing ...

(*Sings again.*)

Grand players may come and grand players may go / But we'll not find the likes of the Gallant John-Joe ...

Scene Six

(*Drinks from large bottle, then moves to centre.*)

Walls is made of bricks and mortar but there's more to them nor that. Watch them long enough and you'll see them turn to wisps – wisps of an hallucination like you were in residence in the middle of a bog ... I was easy, I wasn't easy. Who fathered the chirpaun? Wouldn't go away. It was there – brangling non-stop. And more – it was in the nature of a shadow obscuring the light of day. And didn't I make a jump! Says I to meself – 'Is there any medicine'll cure the like? No,' says I, 'How can pills and potions clarify a shadow between you and the light?' I got up. Pitched the bastarding pills into the fire. Well, if I did – a flame rose – I marked it, I marked it all right – a flame rose, black and amber it was. And it's like that spout of flame is saying, 'You're not outa the wood yet, Mister. You'll be howling for us pills soon enough, never fret!' I should have took that warning more serious – but does anyone? You have to wait for the dunt. And the dunt won't fail you! I comes down this morning, foosthers about for a while. Eleven o'clock – ne'er a sign of family life. Try the bedroom. Empty! She's gone. Me daughter's gone! I knew, you see, on the spot. I just knew. I knew in advance. I ask around – the neighbours, the shop – No. Seen by nobody. The Hitmatist? No. Not in them latitudes – which I knew she wouldn't be. Boss-Man's no help – can't prevent himself postulating and speculating and speechifying. I went down to the Guards the second day. Carrying me load of reservations for having anything to do with them cabbages in uniform. Appear there and you're accused of some crime! I was hardly in the door when the Criminal Investigation of John-Joe Concannon was in full swing. 'What, Mister, do you know about the event? Was your daughter in a disturbed state? How would you describe your own state, right now, and across a succession of recent years?' 'Silent, that's how I'd describe it! Ye'll get nothing outa me.' And, daughter still missing, I slams the barrack door, leaving them Mohawks to their own advices.

(*He settles himself in the story-chair.*)

Day or two after – call from the station. Jacinta Concannon's incarcerated in the Big House for mental patients – admitted of her own accord. Or, anyways, that's the version of events presented to me by the forces of law and order. So I proceeds to visit me daughter, now a registered patient in the care and custody of this State. I find it easy to gain admission – suspicious easy. She's sitting in the ward. Doctors, nurses, warders, none in sight, begod – prominent absentees.

(*He rises and moves to centre ...*)

'Maybe,' says I to meself, 'there's more nor Jacinta's under observation here.' Them institutions is alive with loopholes, false windows, spy-slots and recording apparatuses of all descriptions.

(Comes forward to confide in the audience.)

You're now saying this man has a Prosecution Complex – but before long, matter of fact, I was proved right.

(He brings the story-chair downstage centre, settles ...)

Anyways, Jacinta's sitting there. 'I'm back,' says she, and introduces me to her new-found friend, the White-Be-Night. The White-Be-Night's a dog, and there she is, pattin' the dog. Only bother is the dog's invisible! She's patting thin air. 'Pa,' says she, 'say hello to the White-Be-Night, see what he makes of you. He's the boy'll tell you if you're in your health or no. He has a nose like none other ever was, wherever he got it he's not saying. Just smiles, Pa, with his eyes – no faking that.' And her stroking the head of a dog – that's not there. Sweet suffering Jazus! O, sweet suffering Jazus and his weeping and afflicted Mother but I was a frightened man. I could hardly take it in – what was happening – never mind deal with it. You couldn't credit it unless you saw it fornenst you. Somehow I kept a grip, and says I to meself, 'Reason with her, John-Joe, soother her, things could settle. Reason with her.' And I did. That's exactly what I done. 'All right, Jacinta,' says I, 'it's all right. You vanish from sight – driving us all abstracted – so no one knows are you alive or dead – and you turn up when you fancy. I don't mind. Thing is – you're back. That's what matters. It's all right.' 'Is it, Pa?' sez she. 'That's what I'm saying, daughter. You here safe and sound is the main thing.' 'Pa, are you a-feard of me dog?' Jazus! The dog again. 'He's no dog to be afraid of,' says she. 'Maybe stand in awe of – but that's a different thing altogether.' And I go barsack!

(*He rises, thundery.*)

'Jacinta! Did you listen to a single solitary word I said? Ye rip ye! You're so thick into yourself you're as interested in what I'm saying as the Rock of Muff. Stir yourself, will you? Get up off your Royal Irish rump and take the world by the hasp before it makes bits of you. Are you listening to me?' No response. She could be on the Moon, Neptune, or the approaches to Jupiter. 'Where's that flea-bitten mongrel with the mange?' says I. I made a rush, grabbed that invisible dog and away with me down the tiled corridor.

(*He exits, carrying the invisible dog ... Pause and he re-enters.*)

I waits a few minutes, lands back. 'I hanged the fucker,' says I, 'Did you hear him squealing? Not but he was hard to quench. Hanged him and still he wouldn't give in. Took the mitts to his thrapple – and, bejazus, he's still twitching. Long latter end I had to kick the daylights out of him and the job's a good one. And you needn't worry – he won't be left lying around. I'll turf him into the lake this evening, let the misfortunate eels gluttonize themeslves for a week.' You wouldn't credit her next leap. What does she do only turn into the dog – goes for me – teeth barred – barking, frothing. 'All right, me lady,' says I, 'get this into your loaf. I'll have you certified! I'll have you certified, you bitch you! If the papers has to be signed, I'll put me name to them and let the whole pack say what they like. Someone has to put down the foot or we're all for the black of the bog-hole.' At which point, a swarm of medical staff – as expected – lights on me from th'other side of harmless-looking hospital screens and Jacinta Concannon's father is bodily removed from that institution, with warnings attached concerning future behaviour!

Scene Seven

(He goes to the mangle, takes up the small bottle of medicine, hesitates, decides against it ... takes pills instead, followed by slug from the big bottle – all this to distracted mutterings concerning medical practitioners in general and Baldy Hippocrates in particular ... reprise of scratching the lumbar region, and he sits on the story-chair, resumes.)

So Jacinta Concannon's in the Big House. And her abused father banned from visiting. Beyond that, all I'm told is – tuck back your lugs for this now – no child, no chirpuan! They checked her out – no bun in the oven. Jazus, after all the Crucifixions and the ten Gardens of Agonies I went through! ... What class of a world are we staggering about in at all? Phantoms, is it? Figments? Threads of the mist spun out of a daughter's imaginings, and formented by the fructifrying presence of Cunty Mac Fuck The Chinee ... It's my belief the rot commenced first day she went to work in that chipper, her temper changed, her gestures – her nature somehow smirched. I couldn't ask her direct. 'What's going on down there, Jacinta? Tell me, I'm your father, I'll understand, I'll take steps.' Only I held back. A mistake. A bad mistake. But not a blunder beyond making up for. I said it before – you must listen to thunder – the thunder in the blood. Don't listen, it'll deafen you. Meaning what? Meaning I took steps. Concerning? You know the answer. Concerning me Rickshaw Casanova –

(He rises and moves to central position.)

Mister Prime Suspect from under the Great Wall. What steps did I take? Mind your own business. Them what asks no questions is them what's told no lies. Let nobody say he wasn't warned. Something had to be done. I'll go this far – and, by the way, without admission of anything – I'll admit nothing, I learned that much from what passes for education in this country ... Where was I? ... Yes – this – I didn't make the lakes around here, God Almighty made them. And they're available for all kinds of purposes.

(He moves upstage to the mangle, works the wheel, and sings.)

Grand players may come and grand players may go / but we'll not find the likes of the gallant John-Joe ...

(He makes a knocking sound on the mangle ...)

Knock on the door. The Sergeant begod! Someone missing. Who is it this time? The Chinee! 'Happens every day of the week,' says I. 'People goes missing. No one knows what gets into them. Just get up and go missing. Like going to work.' And he's standing there listening to me, face on him as long as a Lurgan spade. 'Just making a few low-profile enquiries,' says he. 'You don't mind if I call back tomorrow?' 'I'm here regular, Sergeant,' says I. And he departs, the number ten boots squeaking against his bunions.

(He pauses, pleasure in the pause as he reflects on these events ... he moves to centre.)

Well, I'll tell youze one thing and I'll tell youze no more – I won't be organizing no pilgrimages to Knock for Comrade Lee Chang Woo's repose and peace of mind.

Scene Eight

I was clear on one thing only. They might ban me from the premises but I'd visit her all the same. I was going to say hello to me daughter. So I heads for the Big House. According to Boss-Man who has it from Mr Devine who has it from some croony, no doubt, she just sits there and talks. Seems the crowd in charge is making great play of the dog, the White-Be-Night. A wheen of enquiries on that subject. 'Where'd that dog come from?' they want to know. 'I asked for him and he appeared,' says she. 'I heard once on the radio – or maybe from a tree – if you have the animals on your side there's none'll best you.' And she spends hours praying, I'm told, that some animal, the like of her dog, 'll land at John-Joe's feet and stick by him, lend him, one way or another, the lick of courage or hope or belief that the lowest of the low needs to shift one foot after the other and the black load swelling out of all magnitude.

(He views the black invisible load, hovering in the vicinity ... lets it be.)

So there I am in the environs of the Big House. The size of that place – leagues of it. I didn't get into the building, didn't manage that – they've sentries everywhere – I was drove back with a caution. But it must have been she knew somehow I was in the vicinity. They're marching me out of the grounds, and don't I spot her at a high window. She's waving – and I wave back – and I stop and we have this conversation. I stood me ground, hoodlums trying to hustle me outa the place – I stood me ground. 'How are you, Jacinta?' says I. 'Grand, Pa, grand.' 'What do you be thinking of up there, Jacinta?' 'Thinking of?' 'Aye. What does be going on in your head, child?' 'I does be thinking of the one song,' says she. 'What song would that be now?' says I. 'I'll tell you, Pa. You see, I believe a body has just the one song – each particular body – and the trick, if you can learn it, is to sing it, Pa. Then you're floating, then you're flying, then you've wings'll never fail.' And she's gone. I'm outside on the footpath. Gates clanged behind me.

(He wanders irresolutely ... finds an anchor.)

There's strange things happens – every day of the week. The clock in that kitchen, put a lot of money out for it, luminous dial and all. That clock stopped the exact hour Jacinta went out the door – her big departure when she disappeared for good and all. A quarter past nine, a Thursday, last Thursday week. I looked at that clock and I said – 'Christ protect me.' And I wondered should I leave it as it was until the day Jacinta lands back here in the full of her health. No. I lugs it to the clocks-and-watches man below in the town, Joe Armstrong. Who opens it up. 'What happened this clock?' says he. 'How would I know?' says I. 'Beyond repair,' says Armstrong. 'It's like the insides of it was in a traffic accident of odious velocities – resulting in a write-off.' And he closed it up. Now it's back on the dresser. Time? Quarter past nine last Thursday week. Jesus, spare me.

Scene Nine

(He retreats to the mangle-chair, sits.)

Meantime, I'm mainly sticking to the house. I wouldn't satisfy the hoors. I knows the sulphuric tongues of this town – the sideways looks and the halfway gawks. 'Did you hustle her out, John-Joe?' 'Was she drove to it by a hard father?' 'E'er a sign of The Chinee?' I could hear it curdling in their lugs. I was buffeted in the temples listening to rumour, detractions, allegations and calumniations. I'd have given me arms and legs for a bit of peace and quiet. Of course, Boss-Man arrives, fresh from shaving, spewing questions and streaming advice. 'Go easy now,' says I, 'on the bruised and the bet in their woebegone solitudes.' 'I merely called to see how is Jacinta,' says he. 'How would I know,' says I, 'I'm only the father of the party in question.'

(He rises, warming to the fray.)

'But I can tell you this, Boss-Man. Jacinta, just like her father, is surrounded. Surrounded by praying mantises. And you – you're leading the posse. You wanted to bring her on a cruise, didn't you?' 'Yes,' says he, 'for the good of her health.' 'Health, me bollocks,' says I, 'for the good of her curvatures! I heard your offer – holiday heaven and pour-on lingeries. I'm not the ourangatang lots takes me for, you know.' 'You're upset, Concannon,' says he. 'You simply must get out and about, get yourself some fresh air.' 'Right,' says I, 'and be cross-examined. Why'd you sign her in? When'll you sign her out? What's the ailment? Give us the whole story, full slate, nothing less, and remember, we're the ones 'll know if you're holding back anything. Keep that in mind, Mister!' 'You're hysterical, Concannon,' says he, 'that's not the road to Mecca.' 'No,' says I, 'it's the Old Bog Road –'

(*He snarl-sings a phrase from the song.*)

I'm slavin' here on Broadway – this sham-shite harvest morn – I don't want the road to Mecca.

(*He sits.*)

In the dock – numbered inmate in the House of Pariahs – John-Joe Concannon has his own road stretching in front of him – the pack at his heels – and no question under God's heaven of side-stepping the scourgin' that's destined to be.

(*Stares audience.*)

Did y'ever read the Bible? Ever read about the famous escape-goat in the Bible? Did you? Could be they has it in the Koran too, Boss-Man, a grand book, I'm certain sure is in your possession. Mahomet wrote it. The story of the famous escape-goat. If a jug falls – breaks – all spilt, it wasn't the wind done it – you need your escape-goat. Right? Right. Gather the stones – there's a pack of youze in it – gather the stones. Now you're thrashing! Finger your victim – no bother – always one handy. The sun never rose a day yet there wasn't one waiting the call. Grand! Drive your chosen to the cross-roads spot, lots of bawling and shouting to whip up bile and blister. Aye, and the screeching of youze when youze start the stoning. Are you there, Boss-Man, are you there the lot of youze? Are youze comfortable in the cosy of your crossroads crowd? Are youze furnished with your stones? Lift your arms now ...

(Hat off, he moves to kneeling position, centre stage.)

Fire them. Flail them. Peg them. Throng them. Till the victim drops, pulp and flitters of skin. Then youze are free to go home, leave the crossroads its cargo. Home with youze now, scrub your paws, sleep your fill and wake the morrow. And that's the famous story of the escape-goat from outa the Bible.

(He rises ... Silence allowed to breathe ... moves to mangle ... sits on mangle-chair.)

Felt more in meself after that outburst. Bedamnable story – the famous escape-goat.

(Under his breath now.)

Grand players may come and grand players may go / But we'll not find the likes of the gallant John-Joe ...

(Steadying himself, he addresses the audience.)

Commandant John-Joe Reilly was an army man through and through. And, playing football for the army, took a belt in the kidneys that went wrong on him. He was removed to the army hospital, and from there to the coffin, and coffin only goes one place. November, nineteen and fifty-two. Attended the funeral – threw clay on the six-by-two, hear the rattle of it yet. God be with you, John-Joe.

(He positions himself by the mangle, stoically, and sings.)

In each corner of Breiffne there's sorrow and pain / Such a great-hearted sportsman we'll ne'er see again / Grand players may come and grand players may go / But we'll not find the likes of the gallant John-Joe ...

(He rises from the mangle chair ... comes downstage.)

Could I tell youze something else? In the wind-up, you have to get out ...

(Pause.)

I see, says the blind man, and he couldn't see at all ... Met this fella on the street ...

(He gets the story-chair, brings it to central position, sits.)

One of the Wrestler Reillys – the big lump – Hyacinth – wherever he got that for a handle – did they think he was a prescription or what? Anyways, he dribbles up to me below in the Market Square and says he, wheezing, 'Tell me something, is John-Joe Concannon still in it?' 'I believe so, Hyacinth,' says I, 'I think I seen him outside the post office yesterday.'

(Pause.)

'For that matter, could be it wasn't John-Joe I seen at all. Misidentifications is frequent with the weight of years and other pressing commiserations. Could be I was mistaken. Yes, could be ...'

(He rises to loose his final defiant anthem.)

'But I'll tell you where I did see the party in question – for sure and certain. I seen that man John-Joe Concannon standing on a footpath in the vicinity of the Big House – and his eye on a window – his incarcerated daughter, Jacinta, being visible in that high nest with a canopy of blue curtains. And a conversation progressing between the two – every word audible and chiming – clear as a morn in May – every solitary word. It was a conversation of a private nature that few – few enough now, my opinion – might understand. The Chinee came into it – how'd you keep him out? The slopey Hitmatist, Boss-Man the Bountiful, and, to be sure, the famous dog, the brave White-Be-Night – and his abrupt departure from this world – though she'd claim he could never be put down. And the chirpaun, of course, the Phantom of the Opera, God bless him, that never was. Aye. Nothing disputatious, a pair, father an' daughter, in fair harmony over chapter and verse ... Aye ... And then – like talk between many's the father, many's the daughter, just gabbing ... Gabbing of the times was in it, and the times to come, and the day before the races out at Tangmalangmaloo ...

(Slow fade.)